Instant Pot Fish & Seafood Cookbook

77 Healthy& Delicious Instant Pot Recipes for Your Family

Alex Baker

Why You Should Read This Book

Are you always looking for new and healthy cooking methods? Are you interested in discovering new kitchen appliances that can make your cooking in the kitchen seamless and a lot easier? Are you one of the people who love seafood dishes, but never get them well prepared?

If your answers to the above questions are in the affirmative, then this is the cookbook you need. This is because, this cookbook will help shine light on your path to discovering a magnificent tool that will allow you prepare delicious and very healthy fish and seafood dishes for you and all your loved ones!

You want to know more? Let's get started.

This great cookbook will become your new best friend in thekitchen. You will adore it!

This sounds promising and really great, doesn't it?

"Instant Pot Fish & Seafood Cookbook: 77 Healthy& Delicious Instant Pot Recipes for Your Family" is much more than a recipe collection. It's a cooking journal that teaches you everything you need to know about cooking fish and other kinds of seafood using instant pots. In this cookbook, you will discover why you should consider eating more fish and seafood, and also learn more aboutinstant pots and the best ways to use them.

So, don't hesitate! Get your hands on this special cookbook and start cooking!

"Instant Pot Fish & Seafood Cookbook: 77 Healthy&

Delicious Instant Pot Recipes for Your Family" was specially developed to suit all that you need in making that delicious meal and to provide you with all the help you need in the kitchen when it comes to trending, instant and delicious meals! It will be so much fun all the way! You only need to trust us!

Table Of Contents

Chapter 1: The benefits of fish and seafood

Why should you consume more fish and seafood? Why is seafood so highly recommended by nutrition specialists? The answers to these questions are simple and not far-fetched because:

- Consumption of seafood is extremely healthy and provides multiple benefits.
- Seafood contains healthy fats like omega 3, fatty acids and proteins that are very important for your dietary needs.

From the above, it will be unseemly to say that eating more fish and seafood cannot turn out to be one of the best decisions you'll ever make as regards your diet. As a matter of fact, these kind of foods will not only improve your health in one way, but also in so many different ways.

Also, seafood is full of important vitamins like vitamin A, D and the B's complex. And these vitamins have been proven to improve our health, metabolism, immune system and in the long run, our general wellbeing.

Similarly, seafood contains nutrients that will keep your heart functioning healthily, keep your bone growing as expected and improve your mental focus as well.

The omega 3 fatty acids found in fish and seafood can helpmaintain a great eyesight, and also fight conditions like arthritis or rheumatism.

Seafood will not only make you feel great, but will also make you look amazing! Your skin will glow and it will maintain an optimal level of hydration and moisture. You will look young, beautiful and without any blemish, notwithstanding your age.

If you do not find the above as enough reasons to eat seafood, then here comes another:

These special and delicious foods (seafood) will also help you stay happy! Don't laugh! It's true! This is because the compounds found in this kind of foods prevents depression, sadness and other similar state of mind.

Are you now convinced that eating seafood and fish is a good thing to do?

If so, then it's time for you to learn how to choose the best seafood products!

First of all, let's talk about buying fresh fish and seafood. It is important for you know that these products must be firm and full of flesh. There is no point buying them if they smell funny. You must also take note of the fact that, to prevent fresh fish from decaying, the fish should be kept in crushed ice. Therefore, if you purchase fresh fish and seafood, you must consume them within 2 days from the purchase date! If you won't eat these products right away, the best bet is to freeze them.

For already frozen fish and seafood, you need to apply another method to preserve them from decay. So, when you purchase already frozen fish and seafood, make sure it is properly frozen. Majorly, it must be wrapped in a moisture proof package. Don't defreeze this kind of product at room temperature and never refreeze it.

To defreeze it, it will be enough to simply place the frozen fish and seafood under cold water.

Oysters must always be alive when you purchase them. As a matter of fact, they remain alive for 10 days if you keep them in your fridge at 40 degrees F. To know if an oyster is fresh, it must have a creamy color and it must also have a clear liquid. Take note that Oysters are not meant to be freeze.

Shrimp is probably one of the most popular seafood productsavailable. To know if a shrimp is fresh, it must be firm and have some odor (not unpleasant).

Raw shrimp that is still in its shell can be frozen for a longer time than already cooked and frozen ones.

Lobsters must be alive and active when you purchase them. Make sure their tails are curl. This is how you can tell whether they're fresh or not.

Crabs should also be alive when you purchase them. They should be odorless. If you purchase frozen crabs, make sure they are completely frozen.

Crabmeat should be consumed within 3 days from the purchase date and it should be kept in the fridge and on ice until you use it.

We are sure all these advice will come in handy someday,somehow and they will help you get the best fish and seafoodproducts available in the market.

You'll see!

Chapter 2: How to use the instant pot and safety measures

Why are instant pots so popular all over the world?Let's find out!

When we talk about the future of kitchen, instant pots are this future we refer to. Of course, you will need some time to dig your way around these appliances, but once you can dig it, instant pots will become a very important part of your life.

Instant pots will help you prepare tasty dishes in a much more effective way. Just so you know, your foods will maintain their natural textures and flavors and they will be cooked in a healthier way with instant pots.

With instant pots, spending long hours in the kitchen on your food will be a thing of the past.Also, with instant pots, you can forget about complex cooking methods or special skills.

Lastly, with instant pots, you can forget about using a lot of pans and pots for your food.Your success in the kitchen is definitely guaranteed if you choose to purchase and use instant pots!

Instant pots are programmed, with settings and buttons which after you've learnt how to use them, you will have a smooth ride in preparing your food. Yes, it is essential that you should learn how to operate the device. However, if you feel like you do not want to learn so much stuff, then you can use the manual button. Though this is not without its own challenges.

More importantly, you must ensure that you clean your instant pot after using it. And sincerely, instant pots are very easy to clean and get ready for use subsequently.

It is also important for you to know that instant pots functionbased on the ingredients you use. When using instant pots, make sure your ingredients are sliced into the same size, then sauté them brown before cooking them in the pot.

Also, ensure you use at least 1 cup of water when you are cooking in your instant pot. This is very important, and you should not use your instant pot otherwise.

Now that you are equipped with useful tips on how you can use your instant pot, it behooves on us to switch focus to what really matters which is cooking fish and seafood in your instant pot.

If you want to cook your fish and seafood in instant pots, then you need to pay attention to the following.

Generally, your fish and seafood will cook very fast if you use an instant pot, and more importantly, their natural taste andnutrient will be retained. As a result of this, you will obtain amoist and tender dish.

You can choose to steam your fish and seafood or you can opt for stewing. If you choose to stew your fish and seafood, ensure you use some liquid. Also, as soon as the time is up, you must release the pressure from the pot. This is because if you fail to do so, your food may harden and lose its softness.

Here are some guidelines you should follow when cooking fish and seafood in your instant pot:

Seafood and Fish	(Fresh) Cooking Time	(Frozen) Cooking Time
Crab	3 – 4 min.	5 – 6 min.
Whole Fish	5 – 6 min.	7 – 10 min.
Fish fillets	2 – 3 min.	3 – 4 min.
Fish steaks	3 – 4 min.	4 – 6 min.
Lobster	3 – 4 min.	4 – 6 min.
Mussels	2 – 3 min.	4 – 5 min.
Seafood soup	6 – 7 min.	7 – 9 min.
Shrimp	1 – 2 min.	2 – 3 min.

We sincerely hope you will pay attention to this chart anytime youwant to cook fish and seafood in your instant pot.

Now, let's get to the fun part in making irresistibly tasting fish andseafood dishes using your instant pot!You have all you need in your hands right now, so here is sayingwelcome to a never-ending culinary trip of your lifetime!Have fun and enjoy the best and most popular instant pot seafoodand fish recipes!

Chapter 3. The Best 77 Healthy And Delicious Instant Pot Fish And Seafood Recipes

Fish Fillets And Delicious Orange Sauce

You've really got to try this amazing and delicious fish dish! The combination of ingredients is absolutely divine and you will really appreciate it! Trust us!

Preparation time: 10 minutes
Cooking time: 10 minutes
Servings: 4

Ingredients:

4 spring onions, finely chopped
1 inch ginger piece, grated
1 tablespoon olive oil
4 white fish fillets
Juice from 1 orange
Zest from 1 orange
A pinch of salt and black pepper
1 cup fish stock

Directions:

Season fish with salt and pepper, rub them with the oil and

place on a plate for now.

Put ginger, orange juice, orange zest, onions and stock in your instant pot.

Add the steamer basket and place fish fillets inside.

Cover the pot and cook fish on High for 10 minutes.

Release the pressure fast, divide fish on plates, top with the orange sauce from the pot and serve.

Enjoy!

Healthy Steamed White Fish

If you are looking for a very healthy fish based dish you can make in your instant pot, then this is definitely the right one! You will enjoy some pretty amazing flavors and textures!

Ingredients:

4 white fish fillets
1 tablespoon olive oil
1 teaspoon thyme dried
1 pound cherry tomatoes, halved
1 cup black olives, pitted and chopped
A pinch of sea salt and black pepper
1 garlic clove, minced
1 cup water

Directions:

Put the water in your instant pot, place the steamer basket on top and arrange fish inside.

Season with salt, pepper, thyme and garlic.

Add oil, olives and tomatoes, rub gently, cover your instant pot and cook on Low for 10 minutes.

Release the pressure fast, divide fish and all veggies on plates and serve hot.

Enjoy!

Delicious Fish Curry

Have you ever tried such a tasty and exotic dish? Combine the ingredients suggested by us and you'll obtain one of the most delicious Indian curries ever!

Preparation time: 5 minutes
Cooking time: 15 minutes
Servings: 6

Ingredients:

1 tomato, chopped
6 white fish fillets, cut in chunks
2 red bell peppers, cut in thin strips
2 yellow onions, chopped
2 garlic cloves, minced
14 ounces canned coconut milk
1 tablespoon coriander, dried
6 curry leaves
1 tablespoon ginger, minced
2 tablespoons lemon juice
1 teaspoon fenugreek, ground
A pinch of red chili flakes, crushed
½ teaspoon turmeric powder
2 teaspoons cumin, ground
A pinch of salt and black pepper

Directions:

Put the oil in your instant pot and set it on Sauté mode.

Heat the oil up, add curry leaves and fry them for 1 minute.

Add garlic, ginger and onion, stir and sauté for 2 minutes more.

Add cumin, coriander, turmeric, pepper flakes and fenugreek, stir and cook for another 2 minutes.

Add fish, bell peppers, tomatoes and coconut milk, stir, cover the pot and cook on Low for 5 minutes.

Release the pressure for about 10 minutes, uncover the pot, season curry with salt and pepper and divide into serving bowls.

Add lemon juice on top and serve right away.

Enjoy!

Elegant Cod

This is a Mediterranean style fish based dish that you will adore for sure! It's because of the special combination of ingredients! Just check out this amazing recipe and be surprised!

Preparation time: 5 minutes
Cooking time: 10 minutes
Servings: 4

Ingredients:

1 garlic clove, minced
1 tablespoon olive oil
17 ounces cherry tomatoes, halved
4 cod fillets, boneless
2 tablespoons capers, chopped
1 cup black olives, pitted and chopped
Salt and black pepper
1 tablespoon parsley, finely chopped

Directions:

In a heat proof bowl, mix tomatoes with salt, pepper and parsley and toss to coat.
Add oil, fish, olives, capers and garlic, place the bowl in the steamer basket in your instant pot.Cover and cook on High for 7 minutes.
Release the pressure for about 10 minutes, divide fish and veggies on plates and serve right away.
Enjoy!

Unbelievable Cod

You will love this amazing and super tasty dish and you will make it over and over again! Just trust our recommendation and make this great cod today!

Preparation time: 10 minutes
Cooking time: 5 minutes
Servings: 4

Ingredients:

10 ounces peas
1 tablespoon parsley, chopped
4 cod fillets, boneless
1 teaspoon oregano, dried
9 ounces white wine
2 garlic cloves, minced
1 teaspoon paprika
A pinch of sea salt and black pepper

Directions:

Put parsley, paprika, oregano and garlic in your food processor and blend really well.
Add wine, blend again, transfer to a bowl and leave aside.
Put the steamer basket in your instant pot and place fish fillets in the basket.
Season fish with salt and pepper, cover pot and cook on High for 2 minutes.
Release pressure and transfer fish to plates.

Put peas in the steamer basket, cover and cook them on High for 2 minutes.

Release the pressure again and divide peas next to fish.

Add the vinaigrette you've made at the beginning on top and serve.

Enjoy!

Light Salmon Dish

This healthy and delicious poached salmon is all you need after a hard day at work! It will really surprise you with it's incredible taste! The best thing about this dish besides the taste is the fact that it's going to be ready in to time if you use your instant pot!

Preparation time: 5 minutes
Cooking time: 5 minutes
Servings: 4

Ingredients:

4 medium salmon fillets, boneless and skin on
1 bay leaf
1 teaspoon fennel seeds
4 scallions, chopped
Zest from 1 lemon, grated
1 teaspoon white vinegar
3 peppercorns
¼ cup dill, chopped
½ cup white wine
2 cups chicken stock
A pinch of sea salt and black pepper

Directions:

In your instant pot, mix scallions with stock, peppercorns, lemon zest, vinegar, fennel, wine, dill and bay leaf and stir.
Put the steamer basket in your instant pot and arrange salmon fillets inside.

Season the with a pinch of salt and pepper, cover and cook on High for 5 minutes.

Release the pressure fast, uncover your instant pot, divide fish fillets on plates and leave them aside.

Set the pot on Simmer more, cook juices for a couple more minutes, drizzle over salmon and serve right away.

Enjoy!

Special Salmon Dish

This special, crispy and very delicious salmon dish is gong to hypnotize you for sure! Just try it tonight and make everyone happy! The taste is just divine!

Preparation time: 5 minutes
Cooking time: 10 minutes
Servings: 2

Ingredients:

1 cup water
2 medium salmon fillets, skin on
2 tablespoons olive oil
A pinch of sea salt and black pepper

Directions:

Put 1 cup water in your instant pot and place the steamer basket inside.

Put salmon fillets in the steamer basket, season with salt and pepper, cover pot and cook on Low for 3 minutes.

Release the pressure fast, uncover pan and pat dry fish using paper towels.

Heat up a pan with the oil over medium high heat, add fish fillets, cook them for 2 minutes skin side down and divide on plates.

Serve fish with a side salad.

Enjoy!

Superb Salmon And Tasty Rice

It's always amazing to discover new and interesting dishes! Well, this is one of those recipes! You just have to pay attention next and learn how to make this great dish for you and all your loved ones!

Preparation time: 10 minutes
Cooking time: 5 minutes
Servings: 2

Ingredients:

½ cup jasmine rice
A pinch of sea salt and black pepper
2 wild salmon fillets
1 cup chicken stock
½ teaspoon saffron
1 tablespoon butter
½ cup veggie stock mix, dried

Directions:

In your instant pot, mix stock, soup mix, rice, saffron and butter and stir.

Place the steamer basket in your instant pot, place salmon inside, season with salt and pepper, cover and cook on High for 5 minutes.

Release the pressure fast, divide salmon on plates, add rice on the side and serve.

Enjoy!

Amazing Veggies And Wonderful Salmon

This will leave you speechless! It will make you want more and more! Your guests will be really impressed with the taste and the rich flavors!

Preparation time: 10 minutes
Cooking time: 10 minutes
Servings: 2

Ingredients:

1 cinnamon stick
1 tablespoon canola oil
1 cup water
2 salmon fillets, skin on
1 bay leaf
3 cloves
2 cups broccoli florets
1 cup baby carrots
A pinch of sea salt and black pepper
Some lime wedges for serving

Directions:

Put the water in your instant pot and add cinnamon, cloves and bay leaf.

Add the steamer basket to your pot, place salmon inside, season with salt and pepper and brush it with the oil.

Also add carrots and broccoli to the steamer basket, cover instant pot and cook on High for 6 minutes.

Release the pressure fast, uncover pot, divide salmon on plates, add veggies on the side and drizzle the sauce from the pot on top after you've discarded bay leaf, cinnamon and cloves.

Serve this meal with lime wedges on the side.

Enjoy!

Delicious And Spicy Salmon

Make sure you learn how to make this spicy and very flavored dish! This is going to assure your success next time you through a party! Your guests will consider you a star if you choose to cook this spicy salmon dish!

Preparation time: 5 minutes
Cooking time: 10 minutes
Servings: 4

Ingredients:

1 lemon sliced

Juice from 1 lemon

1 cup water

4 medium salmon fillets, boneless and skin on

A pinch of sea salt and black pepper to the taste

2 tablespoons chili peppers, chopped

Directions:

Put 1 cup water in your instant pot and place the steamer basket inside.

Arrange salmon inside the basket, season with salt, pepper and sprinkle chili pepper all over.

Drizzle lemon juice, top fish with lemon slices, cover instant pot and cook on High for 5 minutes.

Release pressure fast, uncover the pot, divide salmon and lemon slices on plates and serve right away.

Enjoy!

Elegant Salmon Dish

If you are in the mood for a special and very sophisticated salmon dish you can prepare in your instant pot, then this is definitely the right place. This next dish is not just delicious! It's also very easy to make at home!

Preparation time: 5 minutes
Cooking time: 15 minutes
Servings: 4

Ingredients:

3 tomatoes, sliced
1 lemon, sliced
4 medium salmon fillets
1 white onion, chopped
4 parsley springs, chopped
4 thyme springs, chopped
3 tablespoons olive oil
2 cups water
A pinch of sea salt and black pepper

Directions:

Spread tomatoes on a parchment paper, season with salt, pepper and drizzle the oil all over.
Add fish fillets on top of tomatoes, also add thyme, onion, lemon slices and parsley.
Wrap everything in parchment paper, and place everything in the steamer basket of your instant pot.
Add 2 cups water to the pot, place steamer basket inside,

cover and cook on Low for 15 minutes.

Release pressure, uncover pot, transfer packet to a working surface, unwrap, divide fish and veggies on plates and serve. Enjoy!

Tasty Salmon Burger

How does this sound? Try something different every day! Now, it's time to make something really delicious: salmon burgers! These taste so great and they will be done in no time.

Preparation time: 10 minutes
Cooking time: 10 minutes
Servings: 4

Ingredients:

1 pound salmon, ground
2 tablespoons lemon zest
Black pepper and a pinch of salt
1 teaspoon olive oil
½ cup panko
Mustard for serving
Tomato slices for serving
Arugula leaves for serving

Directions:

In your food processor, mix salmon with panko, salt, pepper and lemon zest, stir well, shape 4 burgers out of this mix and place them on a plate.

Set your instant pot on Sauté mode, add the oil and heat it up.

Add patties, cover pot and cook on High for 10 minutes.

Release pressure, uncover pot, set it on Sauté mode again and cook burgers for 2 minutes more.

Divide salmon burgers on buns, add tomato slices, arugula and mustard and serve.

Enjoy!

Exceptional White Fish Delight

The name says it all! You will learn how to make an exceptional white fish dish you can serve on a special and elegant occasion! So, let's get to work!

Preparation time: 5 minutes
Cooking time: 25 minutes
Servings: 6

Ingredients:

1 yellow onion, chopped
6 white fish fillets, cut in chunks
Salt and black pepper to the taste
13 ounces potatoes, peeled and cubed
13 ounces milk
14 ounces chicken stock
14 ounces half and half
14 ounces water

Directions:

Put potatoes, fish, onion, milk, stock and water in your instant pot.
Stir everything, cover and cook on High for 10 minutes.
Release the pressure fast, uncover pot, set it on Simmer more, add half and half, salt and pepper, stir and cook for 10 minutes more.
Divide this into serving bowls and enjoy!

Incredible Salmon And Special Raspberry Sauce

How can this get any better? You have the opportunity to discover one of the best and most delicious salmon recipes ever! This dish is very healthy and it tastes divine! Just try it and see for yourself!

Preparation time: 2 hours and 10 minutes
Cooking time: 5 minutes
Servings: 6

Ingredients:

4 leeks, chopped
2 tablespoons olive oil
6 salmon steaks
2 garlic cloves, minced
1 cup clam juice
2 tablespoons parsley, chopped
2 tablespoons lemon juice
1/3 cup dill, chopped
1 teaspoon sherry
A pinch of sea salt
Black pepper to the taste
2 pints red raspberries
1 pint cider vinegar

Directions:

In a bowl, mix raspberries with vinegar and stir well.

Add salmon, stir, cover and keep in the fridge for 2 hours.

Put the oil in your instant pot and set it on Sauté mode.

Add garlic, parsley and leeks, stir and cook for 2 minutes.

Add lemon juice, clam juice, salt, pepper, cherry and dill, stir and cook for 2 minutes.

Add salmon steaks, stir, cover and cook on High for 4 minutes.

Release pressure naturally, divide salmon, leeks and sauce on plates and serve them hot.

Enjoy!

Cod Pudding

You might find this a bit difficult to make but we can assure you that it's very simple. All you have to do is to follow out directions and you will enjoy a tasty and very healthy fish pudding in under 30 minutes.

Preparation time: 10 minutes
Cooking time: 20 minutes
Servings: 4

Ingredients:

2 tablespoons parsley, chopped
1 pound cod fillets, cubed
4 ounces bread crumbs
2 ounces butter
2 eggs, whisked
2 teaspoons lemon juice
Salt and black pepper
½ pint shrimp sauce
½ pint water
½ pint milk

Directions:

In a bowl, mix bread crumbs with salt, pepper, parsley, lemon juice and fish cubes and stir well.
Heat up a pan with the butter over medium high heat, add milk, stir and bring to a simmer.
Put eggs in a bowl and add milk mix over them.

Add this to the bowl with the fish, stir and leave aside everything for a couple of minutes.

Transfer this to a heat proof dish.

Place steamer basket into your instant pot, add the water to the pot, add baking dish inside, cover and cook on High for 15 minutes.

Release pressure fast, uncover, divide cod pudding on plates, drizzle shrimp sauce all over and serve.

Enjoy!

Popular Jambalaya

We are sure you've heard about this great dish! Well, now you can taste it in the comfort of your own home! We recommend you to make this incredible dish on a Sunday when you gather all your friends and family at the table!

Preparation time: 10 minutes
Cooking time: 22 minutes
Servings: 4

Ingredients:

1 pound medium shrimp, peeled and deveined
1 pound chicken breast, skinless, boneless and chopped
2 tablespoons olive oil
1 pound sausage, cooked and chopped
1 and ½ cups rice
2 cups yellow onion, chopped
2 tablespoons garlic, chopped
3 and ½ cups chicken stock
2 cups mixed bell peppers, chopped
1 tablespoon Creole seasoning
1 cup canned tomatoes, crushed
1 tablespoon Worcestershire sauce

Directions:

Set your instant pot on Sauté mode, add chicken pieces, season with Creole seasoning, stir, brown for a couple of minutes on all sides, transfer to a bowl and leave aside for now.

Add the oil to your instant pot, heat it up, add garlic, bell peppers and onions, stir and cook for 2 minutes.

Add rice, stir and cook for 2 minutes more.

Add Worcestershire sauce, tomatoes, stock and chicken, stir, cover and cook on High for 10 minutes.

Release pressure, uncover pot, add shrimp and sausage, stir and cook on High for 2 minutes.

Release pressure fast, divide jambalaya on plates and serve right away.

Enjoy!

Fish And Noodles

This time, let's try something easy to make that's going to be ready in no time! The combination of ingredients is really great and we can assure you that everyone will like it!

Preparation time: 10 minutes
Cooking time: 15 minutes
Servings: 4

Ingredients:

1 tablespoon olive oil
1 and ¼ cups water
1 small red onion, chopped
8 ounces egg noodles
14 ounces canned tomatoes, chopped
A pinch of basil, dried
A pinch of oregano, dried
A pinch of garlic powder
14 ounces canned tuna, dried
A pinch of sea salt
Black pepper to the taste
1 tablespoon parsley, chopped
8 ounces canned artichoke hearts, drained and chopped
Some crumbled feta cheese for serving

Directions:

Add the oil to your instant pot, set it on Sauté mode and heat it up.

Add onion, stir and cook for 2 minutes.

Add noodles, tomatoes, water, salt and pepper, stir, set the pot to Simmer mode and cook for 10 minutes.

Add artichokes and tune, stir, cover pot and cook everything on High for 5 minutes.

Release pressure fast, divide tuna and noodles on plates, sprinkle feta cheese and parsley and serve.

Enjoy!

Tuna Delight

It's always a pleasure to discover new and very interesting recipes! This is one of them! The ingredients you'll use are simple but the result is wonderful! You'll see!

Preparation time: 5 minutes
Cooking time: 5 minutes
Servings: 4

Ingredients:

14 ounces canned tuna, flaked

28 ounces cream of mushroom

15 ounces egg noodles

1 cup peas

3 cups water

¼ cup bread crumbs

4 ounces cheddar cheese, grated

Directions:

Mix noodles and water in your instant pot.

Add cream, tuna and peas, stir, cover and cook on High for 5 minutes.

Release pressure fast, add cheese, stir well and divide the mix on plates.

Sprinkle bread crumbs on to and serve.

Enjoy!

Delicious Mackerel

This is a very healthy fish you should include in your diet! Try making him the way we suggest you and everyone will enjoy it!

Preparation time: 10 minutes
Cooking time: 6 minutes
Servings: 4

Ingredients:

8 shallots, chopped
1 teaspoon shrimp powder
3 garlic cloves, minced
18 ounces mackerel, chopped
1 teaspoon turmeric
2 lemongrass sticks, halved
1 tablespoon chili paste
1 inch ginger, grated
3.5 ounces water
5 tablespoons olive oil
6 laska leaves stalks
1 tablespoon sugar
A pinch of salt
1 tablespoon tamarind paste

Directions:

In a food processor, mix chili paste with shrimp powder, shallots and turmeric and blend well.

Put the oil in your instant pot, set it on Sauté mode and heat it up.

Add the paste you've made, add fish, lemon grass, laska leaves, ginger salt and sugar, stir, cover and sauté for 1 minute.

Mix tamarind with the water, stir well and add this to the pot.

Cover pot and cook on High for 5 minutes.

Release pressure, divide fish on plates and serve.

Enjoy!

Delicious Miso Mackerel

You should give this dish a chance! It's nothing like other recipes you've tried until now! It's really delicious and easy to make and you can try it today!

Preparation time: 10 minutes
Cooking time: 50 minutes
Servings: 4

Ingredients:

1 garlic clove, minced
1 shallot, chopped
1 cup water
2 pounds mackerel, cut in chunks
1/3 cup mirin
1/3 cup sake
1 small ginger piece, chopped
¼ cup miso
1 yellow onion, chopped
2 celery stalks, chopped
1 teaspoon sugar
1 teaspoon hot mustard
1 tablespoon rice vinegar
A pinch of salt

Directions:

Put sake, mirin, garlic, shallot and ginger in your instant pot, set it on Simmer mode and cook for 2 minutes.

Add water, miso and mackerel, stir, cover and cook on High for 45 minutes.

In a bowl, mix vinegar with mustard, sugar and a pinch of salt and whisk well.

Put onion and celery in another bowl, cover with very cold water and leave aside for a couple of minutes.

Drain and add them to the vinegar and mustard mix

Release pressure from the pot, divide mackerel into bowl, top vinegar mix on top and serve.

Enjoy!

Mackerel And Lemon Delight

This recipes requires your full attention! It's simple to make but make sure you follow the directions! Combine the right flavors and your success in the kitchen is guaranteed!

Preparation time: 5 minutes
Cooking time: 10 minutes
Servings: 4

Ingredients:

Juice from 1 lemon
Zest from 1 lemon, grated
4 mackerels
1 tablespoon chives, minced
A pinch of sea salt and black pepper to the taste
1 tablespoon butter
1 egg, whisked
2 tablespoons margarine
1 tablespoon sunflower oil
3 lemon wedges
10 ounces water

Directions:

In a bowl, mix lemon juice with bread crumbs, lemon zest, salt, pepper, chives and egg and stir very well.
Dip mackerels in this mix.
Add the oil and the butter to your instant pot, set it on Sauté mode and heat them up.

Add mackerels, brown them on all sides and transfer them to a plate.

Discard oil and butter and add the water to the pot.

Place the steamer basket in your instant pot.

Grease a baking dish with the margarine, place mackerels in the dish and place the dish in the pot, cover and cook on High for 6 minutes.

Release the pressure fast, divide mackerel on plates and serve with lemon wedges on the side.

Enjoy!

Perfect Mussels

Who doesn't like a tasty mussels dish! The best thing about this dish is that it's going to be ready in only 5 minutes. So, you will be able to enjoy it really soon!

Preparation time: 5 minutes
Cooking time: 5 minutes
Servings: 4

Ingredients:

1 yellow onion, chopped
1 radicchio, chopped
2 pounds mussels, scrubbed
1 pound baby spinach leaves
1 garlic clove, minced
½ cup white wine
A drizzle of olive oil
½ cup water

Directions:

Put the oil in your instant pot, set it on Sauté mode and heat it up.

Add onion and garlic, stir and cook them for 2 minutes.

Add wine and water, stir and place the steamer basket inside as well.

Put the mussels in the pot, cover and cook on High for 3 minutes.

Release pressure and arrange mussels on a platter where you've already arranged spinach and radicchio.

Drizzle the juice from the pot all over and serve mussels right away.
Enjoy!

Napolitano Style Mussels

You just have to try this Mediterranean style mussels dish! All you need to use is your instant pot! It sounds pretty easy, doesn't it?

Preparation time: 10 minutes
Cooking time: 5 minutes
Servings: 4

Ingredients:

2 jalapenos, chopped
1 small yellow onion, chopped
29 ounces canned tomatoes, chopped
¼ cup white wine
¼ cup balsamic vinegar
2 pounds mussels, scrubbed
¼ cup olive oil
2 garlic cloves, minced
A pinch of sea salt
2 tablespoons red pepper flakes
½ cup basil, chopped
Lemon slices

Directions:

Put oil in your instant pot and set it on Simmer mode.
Add tomatoes, jalapenos, onion, wine, garlic, pepper flakes and vinegar, stir and bring to a boil.
Add mussels, stir, cover pot and cook on Low for 4 minutes.

Release pressure fast, add a pinch of salt and basil, divide everything into bowls and serve with lemon slices on the side.

Enjoy!

Spicy Mussels

Did you know you could use some simple mussels to make a rich and textured dish? If you are a fan of spicy combinations, then you should really try this next recipe!

Preparation time: 5 minutes
Cooking time: 4 minutes
Servings: 4

Ingredients:

14 ounces tomatoes, chopped
½ teaspoon red pepper flakes
2 tablespoons olive oil
2 pounds mussels, scrubbed
1 yellow onion, chopped
2 teaspoons oregano, dried
2 garlic cloves, minced
½ cup chicken stock

Directions:

Add the oil to your instant pot, set it on Sauté mode and heat it up.

Add pepper flakes, garlic and onions, stir and cook for 3 minutes.

Add tomatoes, oregano, stock and mussels, stir, cover and cook on Low for 2 minutes.

Release the pressure fast, divide mussels into bowls and serve.

Enjoy!

Mussels And Sausages

Have you ever tried such a combination? Well, maybe it's time you tried something really different and delicious. Today, we recommend you to make this delicious recipe!

Preparation time: 10 minutes
Cooking time: 8 minutes
Servings: 4

Ingredients:

12 ounces beer
2 pounds mussels, scrubbed
1 yellow onion, chopped
1 tablespoon olive oil
1 tablespoon sweet paprika
8 ounces sausage, chopped

Directions:

Put the oil in your instant pot, set it on Sauté mode and heat it up.
Add onion, stir and cook for 2 minutes.
Add sausages, stir and cook for 4 minutes more.
Add mussels, paprika and beer, stir, cover and cook on Low for 2 minutes.
Release pressure, uncover pot and serve into bowls.
Enjoy!

Cioppino

If you are looking for a hearty and delicious meal to prepare tonight, then this cioppino is exactly what you need. This dish is so rich, extremely tasty and you will love it!

Preparation time: 10 minutes
Cooking time: 25 minutes
Servings: 3

Ingredients:

1 and ½ pounds shrimp, peeled and deveined
12 mussels
12 clams
1 cup butter
1 and ½ pounds white fish fillets, cubed
½ cup parsley, chopped
20 ounces canned tomatoes, chopped
2 yellow onions, chopped
2 bay leaves
3 garlic cloves, minced
1 tablespoon basil, dried
8 ounces clam juice
1 and ½ cups white wine
½ teaspoon marjoram, dried
A pinch of sea salt
Black pepper to the taste

Directions:

Put the butter in your instant pot, set it on Sauté mode and melt it.

Add garlic and onion, stir and sauté for 2 minutes.

Add tomatoes, parsley, clam juice, wine, bay leaves, basil, salt, pepper and marjoram, stir, cover and cook on High for 10 minutes.

Release pressure, turn the pot to Sauté mode again, add mussels and clams, stir and cook for 8 minutes.

Add shrimp and fish, stir, cover and cook on High for 3 minutes more.

Serve into bowls.

Enjoy!

Wonderful Clams Delight

You need to try this amazing dish right away! The ingredients are at hand and they combine perfectly! Accompany the dish with some white wine and everything should be perfect!

Preparation time: 10 minutes
Cooking time: 15 minutes
Servings: 4

Ingredients:

2 chorizo links, chopped

15 clams

30 mussels, scrubbed

10 ounces beer

1 yellow onion, chopped

1 pound red potatoes, peeled and halved

1 teaspoon olive oil

2 tablespoons parsley, chopped

Lemon wedges

Directions:

Put the oil in your instant pot, set it on Sauté mode and heat it up.

Add onions and chorizo pieces, stir and cook for 4 minutes.

Add potatoes, clams, mussels and beer, stir, cover and cook on High for 10 minutes.

Release pressure, add parsley, stir, transfer to bowls and serve with lemon wedges.

Enjoy!

Delicious Clams And Parmesan

Feel free to make this amazing dish for a special and romantic dinner! Your loved one will be really impressed.

Preparation time: 10 minutes
Cooking time: 5 minutes
Servings: 4

Ingredients:

3 garlic cloves, minced
24 clams, scrubbed
¼ cup parsley, chopped
4 tablespoons butter
1 teaspoon oregano, dried
¼ cup parmesan, grated
1 cup bread crumbs
Lemon wedges for serving
2 cups water

Directions:

Put 2 cups water in your instant pot and place the steamer basket inside.

In a bowl, mix crumbs with parsley, parm, oregano, garlic and butter and stir really well.

Divide this in opened clams, put them in the steamer basket, cover your instant pot and cook on High for 5 minutes.

Release pressure, divide clams on plates and serve with lemon wedges.

Tasty Crab

This is one of our favorite seafood dishes! Make sure everyone gets to taste some of this amazing dish!

Preparation time: 10 minutes
Cooking time: 3 minutes
Servings: 4

Ingredients:

1 cup water
4 pounds crab legs, halved
¼ cup butter
4 lemon wedges

Directions:

Put the water in your instant pot and add the steamer basket inside.

Put crab legs in the basket, cover and cook on High for 3 minutes.

Release pressure fast, transfer crab legs to a big bowl and butter all over and leave it to melt.

Serve with lemon wedges.

Elegant Shrimp Dish

This is a magical dish that will make you feel good all day long! You will end up loving this great recipe!

Preparation time: 5 minutes
Cooking time: 5 minutes
Servings: 4

Ingredients:

2 tablespoons parsley, chopped
1 cup yellow onion, chopped
1 and ½ pounds shrimp, peeled and deveined
2 tablespoon olive oil
½ cup fish stock
2 teaspoons hot paprika
4 garlic cloves, minced
¼ cup white wine
1 cup tomato sauce
A pinch of saffron
½ teaspoon sugar
1 bay leaf
¼ teaspoon thyme, dried
1 teaspoon hot red pepper, crushed
A pinch of pink salt
Black pepper to the taste

Directions:

Put the oil in your instant pot, set it on Sauté mode and heat it up.

Add shrimp, stir, cook for 1 minute, transfer to a bowl and leave aside for now.

Add onion, stir and sauté it for 2 minutes.

Add wine, garlic, paprika and parsley, stir and cook for 2 minutes.

Add saffron, sugar, stock, tomato, red pepper, bay leaf, thyme, salt and pepper, stir, cover and cook on High for 4 minutes.

Release pressure fast, add shrimp, cover and cook on High for 2 minutes.

Release pressure again, divide everything on plates and serve.

Enjoy!

Amazing Paella

You don't need to be an expert in the kitchen to cook a really tasty and delicious meal for your family! All you need is to pay attention next and learn a new and exciting seafood dish you can make in your instant pot.

Preparation time: 10 minutes
Cooking time: 5 minutes
Servings: 4

Ingredients:

1 cup jasmine rice
20 big shrimp, deveined
A pinch of red pepper, crushed
¼ cup parsley, chopped
A pinch of sea salt
Black pepper to the taste
¼ cup ghee
A pinch of saffron
1 and ½ cups water
Juice from 1 lemon
4 garlic cloves, minced
Cheddar cheese, grated for serving

Directions:

In your instant pot, mix rice with shrimp, ghee, parsley, salt, pepper, red pepper, lemon juice, saffron, garlic and water, stir, cover and cook on High for 5 minutes.

Release pressure, peel shrimps and divide them on plates. Add rice mix on top, parsley and grated cheese and serve. Enjoy!

Shrimp And Sausages

If you've already tried combining mussels and sausages, then you are really going to appreciate this next recipe! So, what are you waiting for? Get all the ingredients and start cooking!

Preparation time: 5 minutes
Cooking time: 5 minutes
Servings: 4

Ingredients:

12 ounces sausage, cooked and sliced

1 and ½ pounds shrimp, deveined

1 tablespoon old bay seasoning

4 ears of corn, each cut in 3 parts

16 ounces beer

A pinch of sea salt

Black pepper to the taste

2 yellow onions, cut in wedges

1 teaspoon red pepper flakes, crushed

8 garlic cloves, minced

1 pound gold potatoes, cut in medium chunks

Directions:

Mix beer with old bay seasoning, pepper flakes, salt, pepper, garlic, onions, potatoes, sausage, corn and shrimp in your instant pot, stir, cover and cook on High for 5 minutes.

Release pressure fast, divide into bowls and serve.

Enjoy!

Amazing Shrimp Curry

If Indian cuisine is one of your favorite ones, then you really need to try this next dish! It will really bring India to your kitchen because of the magnificent flavors!

Preparation time: 5 minutes
Cooking time: 30 minutes
Servings: 4

Ingredients:

1 cinnamon stick
2 bay leaves
1 pound shrimp, deveined and peeled
1/3 cup butter
2 red onions chopped
10 cloves
3 cardamom pods
14 red chilies, dried and crushed
½ cup cashews
1 tablespoon garlic paste
3 green chilies, chopped
1 tablespoon ginger paste
A pinch of sea salt
1 teaspoon sugar
4 tomatoes, chopped
1 teaspoon fenugreek leaves, dried and crushed
½ cup cream

Directions:

Put the butter in your instant pot, set it on Sauté mode and heat it up.

Add cardamom, cinnamon stick, bay leaves and onion, stir and cook for 3 minutes.

Add green chilies, cashews, garlic paste, cloves, ginger paste, red chilies and a pinch of salt, stir, cover and cook on High for 15 minutes.

Release the pressure fast, pour this mix into your food processor and blend well.

Return this to your instant pot, add shrimp, stir, cover and cook on High for 8 minutes.

Release pressure, switch pot to Simmer mode, add cream, sugar and fenugreek, stir and simmer for 5 minutes.Divide on plates and serve hot.

Enjoy!

Tasty Shrimp Dish

It's tasty, full of flavors and rich textures! You should give it a try! Everyone will adore this dish and they will ask for more!

Preparation time: 5 minutes
Cooking time: 6 minutes
Servings: 4

Ingredients:

4 lemon slices
1 cup bouillon
1 pound shrimp, deveined and peeled
1 yellow onion, chopped
¼ cup mushrooms, chopped
½ teaspoon curry powder
2 tablespoons shortening
A pinch of sea salt
Black pepper to the taste
1 cup milk
3 tablespoons white flour
½ cup raisins

Directions:

Put shortening in your instant pot, set it on Sauté mode and heat it up.
Add mushrooms and onion, stir and cook for 2 minutes.
Add curry powder, lemon slices, salt, pepper, bouillon, shrimp and raisins, stir, cover and cook on High for 2

minutes.

In a bowl, mix milk with flour and stir well.

Release pressure from the pot, add milk and flour, stir, switch instant pot to Simmer mode and cook everything until it thickens.

Divide into serving bowls and serve.

Enjoy!

Shrimp With Amazing Dill Sauce

If you decide to make this dish tonight, make sure you have enough for everyone! We are sure that once your guests or family taste this, they will ask for seconds!

Preparation time: 10 minutes
Cooking time: 10 minutes
Servings: 4

Ingredients:

1 small yellow onion, chopped

2 tablespoons olive oil

1 pound shrimp, peeled and deveined

2 tablespoons cornstarch

1 cup white wine

¾ cup milk

1 teaspoon dill, chopped

Directions:

Put the oil in your instant pot, set it on Sauté mode and heat it up.

Add onion, stir and cook for 2 minutes.Add wine and shrimp, stir, cover and cook on High for 2 minutes more.

Release pressure fast, switch pot to Simmer mode, add cornstarch mixed with milk and dill, stir and cook for 5 minutes.Divide into bowls and serve.

Enjoy!

Shrimp Stew

It's a delicious stew you can make at home in under 20 minutes. Even your kids will adore this incredible stew!

Preparation time: 5 minutes
Cooking time: 15 minutes
Servings: 3

Ingredients:

4 tablespoons olive oil
2 pounds shrimp, peeled and deveined
A pinch of sea salt
1 pound tomatoes, peeled and chopped
8 potatoes, peeled and cut in medium chunks
4 yellow onions, chopped
1 teaspoon coriander, dried
1 tablespoon watercress, chopped
Juice from 1 lemon
1 teaspoon curry powder

Directions:

Put some water in your instant pot, place the steamer basket inside, add potatoes, cover and cook on High for 10 minutes.
Release pressure, transfer potatoes to a bowl and leave them to cool down.
Clean up your pot, add the oil, set pot to Sauté mode and heat it up.
Add onion, stir and cook for 4 minutes.Add curry powder,

coriander and salt, stir and cook for 5 minutes more.

Add shrimp, lemon juice, tomatoes and potatoes, stir, cover and cook on High for 3 minutes.

Release pressure, divide stew in bowls and serve with watercress on top.

Enjoy!

Creole Shrimp

You want something delicious for dinner tonight but you are not in the mood to spend long hours in the kitchen? We have the perfect solution for you! grab your instant pot and make a delicious shrimp dish!

Preparation time: 10 minutes
Cooking time: 5 minutes
Servings: 4

Ingredients:

1 cup tomato juice
2 teaspoons vinegar
1 cup shrimp, cooked, peeled and deveined
1 and ½ cup rice, already cooked
A pinch of sea salt
1 teaspoon chili powder
½ teaspoon sugar
1 cup celery, chopped
2 tablespoons olive oil
1 yellow onion, chopped

Directions:

Put the oil in your instant pot, set it on Sauté mode and heat it up.
Add celery and onion, stir and sauté them for 2 minutes.
Add chili powder, salt, vinegar, tomato juice, sugar, rice and shrimp, stir, cover and cook on High for 3 minutes.

Release pressure naturally, divide on plates and serve.
Enjoy!

Unique Shrimp Dish

This is something you've never tried before! It's so amazing and delicious and even your most pretentious guests will appreciate this dish!

Preparation time: 5 minutes
Cooking time: 4 minutes
Servings: 4

Ingredients:

2 tablespoons soy sauce
1 pound shrimp, peeled and deveined
1 cup chicken stock
3 tablespoon sugar
3 tablespoons vinegar
½ pound pea pods
¾ cup pineapple juice

Directions:

In your instant pot, mix shrimp with pea pods, soy sauce, stock, vinegar, pineapple juice and sugar and stir everything well.
Cover pot, cook on High for 4 minutes and release pressure naturally.
Divide into bowls and serve.
Enjoy!

Special Shrimp

You need to try something different every day! That's why we got this special recipe just for you!

Preparation time: 20 minutes
Cooking time: 10 minutes
Servings: 4

Ingredients:

18 ounces shrimp, peeled and deveined
A pinch of sea salt
3 ounces mustard oil
½ tablespoon mustard seeds
1 teaspoon turmeric
2 green chilies, halved lengthwise
4 ounces curs, beaten
2 onions, chopped
1 small ginger piece, grated
Rice, already cooked for serving

Directions:

Put mustard seeds in a bowl, add water, leave aside for 10 minutes, drain and blend in your blender.

In another bowl, mix mustard oil with shrimp, mustard paste, turmeric, onions, salt, chilies, ginger and curd and stir.

Transfer this to your instant pot, cover and cook on Low for 10 minutes.

Release pressure, divide shrimp in bowls and serve with rice. Enjoy!

Italian Shrimp Scampi

It's new, it's original and it will amaze your taste buds! Does this sound good to you? Try this great dish right away!

Preparation time: 10 minutes
Cooking time: 5 minutes
Servings: 4

Ingredients:

10 ounces canned tomatoes, chopped
1 garlic clove, minced
1 pound shrimp, peeled, deveined and cooked
2 tablespoons olive oil
¼ teaspoon oregano, dried
1/3 cup tomato paste
1 cup parmesan, grated
1/3 cup water
1 tablespoon parsley, chopped
Cooked spaghetti for serving

Directions:

Put the oil in your instant pot, set it on Sauté mode and heat it up.
Add garlic, stir and cook for 2 minutes.
Add tomato paste, shrimp, water, tomatoes, parsley and oregano, stir, cover and cook on High for 3 minutes.
Release pressure, divide spaghetti on plates and divide shrimp mix and sprinkle parmesan on top.
Enjoy!

Delicious Flounder And Shrimp

It's an interesting combination and we are sure you will love it! The instant pot will allow you to enjoy your new favorite dish in no time!

Preparation time: 5 minutes
Cooking time: 5 minutes
Servings: 4

Ingredients:

½ pound shrimp, peeled, deveined and cooked
2 pounds flounder
½ cup water
2 tablespoons butter
4 lemon wedges
A pinch of sea salt and black pepper to the taste

Directions:

Put the water in your instant pot and place the steamer basket inside.

Add fish into the basket, season with a pinch of salt and some black pepper, cover and cook on High for 10 minutes.

Release pressure fast, divide fish on plates and leave it to cool down a bit.

Clean you instant pot, add butter, set pot to Sauté mode and heat it up.

Add shrimp, salt and pepper, stir, cook for a couple of seconds and divide on plates next to the fish.

Drizzle the butter all over and serve with lemon wedges on

the side.
Enjoy!

Shrimp Risotto

You won't feel the need to eat anything else all day! This is the best dish ever! It's so rich and delicious!

Preparation time: 10 minutes
Cooking time: 20 minutes
Servings: 4

Ingredients:

2 garlic cloves, minced
4 tablespoons butter, soft
1 and ½ cups Arborio rice
1 yellow onion, chopped
4 and ½ cups chicken stock
1 pound shrimp, peeled and deveined
2 tablespoons white wine
A pinch of sea salt
Black pepper to the taste
¾ cup parmesan, grated
½ cup parsley, chopped

Directions:

Put half of the butter into your instant pot, set it on Sauté mode and heat it up.
Add onion and garlic, stir and cook for 4 minutes.
Add rice, stir and cook for 1 minute more.
Add wine, 3 cups stock, a pinch of salt and black pepper, stir, cover and cook on High fro 10 minutes.

Release pressure, add shrimp, the remaining stock, stir and switch the pot to Simmer mode.Cook everything for 5 minutes, add cheese, the rest of the butter and parsley and stir.

Divide thin on plates and serve right away.

Enjoy!

Delicious And Simple Octopus

Have you ever tried making a seafood salad in your instant pot? Pay attention and learn how to make this next one! It's so exotic and delicious!

Preparation time: 5 minutes
Cooking time: 35 minutes
Servings: 6

Ingredients:

2 pounds potatoes
2 pound octopus, head discarded, tentacles separated
1 bay leaf
½ teaspoon peppercorns
3 garlic cloves
Some water
2 tablespoons parsley, chopped
2 tablespoons olive oil
A pinch of sea salt
Black pepper to the taste
5 tablespoons vinegar

Directions:

Put some water in your instant pot, add potatoes, stir, cover and cook them on High for 15 minutes.
Release pressure, transfer potatoes to a bowl, cool them down, peeled and chop them.
Clean your instant pot, add octopus, some water to cover, 1

garlic clove, bay leaf, a pinch of salt and peppercorns, stir, cover and cook on High for 20 minutes.

Release pressure, drain octopus, chop and add this to the potatoes bowl.

In a separate bowl, mix the rest of the garlic with oil, vinegar, a pinch of salt and pepper and whisk well.

Add this to your salad, sprinkle parsley, toss to coat and serve.

Enjoy!

Tasty Gumbo

This is so fun to make and it tastes delicious! You need to make it today and enjoy it as much as you can!

Preparation time: 5 minutes
Cooking time: 25 minutes
Servings: 10

Ingredients:

1 cup green bell pepper, chopped
½ cup celery, chopped
1 and ¼ cup white flour
¾ cup vegetable oil
1 cup yellow onion, chopped
3 bay leaves
A pinch of cayenne pepper
2 tablespoons peanut oil
6 plum tomatoes, chopped
½ teaspoon garlic powder
½ teaspoon onion powder
1 teaspoon celery seeds
1 teaspoon thyme, dried
1 pound sausage, chopped
1 teaspoon sweet paprika
2 quarts chicken stock
24 oysters
24 crawfish tails
24 shrimp, peeled and deveined

½ pound crabmeat

A pinch of sea salt

Black pepper to the taste

Directions:

Heat up a pan with the vegetable oil over medium high heat, add flour, stir very well, cook for 4 minutes and take off heat.

Put peanut oil into your instant pot, set it on Sauté mode and heat it up.

Add peppers, onion, celery and garlic, stir and sauté them for 10 minutes.

Add stock, sausage, tomatoes, cayenne, onion powder, garlic powder, thyme, bay leaves, paprika and celery seeds, stir and cook for 3 minutes.

Add flour mix, crawfish, crabmeat, shrimp, salt, pepper and oysters, stir, cover and cook on High for 15 minutes.

Release pressure, divide gumbo into bowls and serve.

Enjoy!

Portuguese Seafood Stew

This is a special recipe we found just for you! Prepare it today and make everyone really happy! It's so delicious and amazing!

Preparation time: 24 hours
Cooking time: 15 minutes
Servings: 4

Ingredients:

1 cup red wine
1 big octopus, prepared
1 cup water
1 cup white wine
½ cup olive oil
½ cup sunflower oil
1 tablespoon hot sauce
2 teaspoons pepper sauce
1 tablespoon paprika
½ bunch parsley, chopped
A pinch of sea salt
Black pepper to the taste
1 tablespoon tomato sauce
4 potatoes, peeled and cut in quarters
1 yellow onion, finely chopped
2 garlic cloves, minced

Directions:

In a bowl, mix red and white wine with water, sunflower oil, hot sauce, pepper sauce, tomato paste, paprika, salt, pepper and parsley and stir.

Add octopus, toss to coat well and keep in the fridge for 1 day.

Add the olive oil to your instant pot, set it on Sauté mode and heat it up.

Add potatoes and onions, stir and cook them for 3 minutes.

Add octopus, its marinade, stir, cover and cook on High for 8 minutes.

Release pressure, divide stew into bowls and serve right away.

Enjoy!

Mediterranean Octopus Dish

This is not just very tasty and easy to make! This Greek dish is also very light and it can be done really fast! You will become a star if you make this dish!

Preparation time: 10 minutes
Cooking time: 15 minutes
Servings: 5

Ingredients:

2 teaspoons oregano, dried
2 rosemary springs
1 octopus, prepared
1 teaspoon black peppercorns
4 thyme springs
1 small yellow onion, chopped
Juice from ½ lemon
3 tablespoons olive oil
For the marinade:
4 garlic cloves, minced
Juice from ½ lemon
¼ cup olive oil
2 thyme springs
A pinch of salt and pepper
1 rosemary spring

Directions:

In your instant pot, mix octopus with 4 thyme springs, 2

rosemary ones, juice from ½ lemon, peppercorns, oregano, onion, a pinch of salt and 3 tablespoons olive oil, stir, cover and cook on Low for 10 minutes.

Release pressure, transfer octopus to a cutting board, cool down, chop and put in a bowl.

Mix octopus pieces with juice from ½ lemon, ¼ cup oil, 1 rosemary spring, garlic, 2 thyme springs, salt and pepper, stir and leave aside for 1 hour.

Place marinated pieces on preheated grill over medium high heat, cook for 3 minutes on each side and serve with the marinade drizzled on top.

Enjoy!

Easy Stuffed Squid

This is very rich and delicious! It's full of amazing flavors and interesting tastes! Why don't you try it today and enjoy its marvelous taste?

Preparation time: 10 minutes
Cooking time: 20 minutes
Servings: 4

Ingredients:

14 ounces dashi stock

4 tablespoons soy sauce

4 squid, tentacles separated and chopped

1 cup rice

2 tablespoons sake

1 tablespoon mirin

2 tablespoons sugar

Directions:

In a bowl, mix tentacles with rice, stir and stuff squid with this mix.

Place stuffed squid in your instant pot, add soy sauce, stock, sugar, sake and mirin, stir, cover and cook on High for 15 minutes.

Release pressure fast, divide squid on plates and serve.

Enjoy!

Tasty Seafood Masala

Make this delicious masala using squid and some other special ingredients you are about to discover! Enjoy it!

Preparation time: 10 minutes
Cooking time: 15 minutes
Servings: 4

Ingredients:

1 and ½ tablespoons red chili powder
17 ounces squid
A pinch of sea salt
Black pepper to the taste
2 cups water
¼ teaspoon turmeric
5 small coconut pieces, shredded
4 garlic cloves, minced
3 tablespoons olive oil
½ teaspoon cumin seeds
1 small ginger pieces, grated
¼ teaspoon mustard seeds

Directions:

In your instant pot, mix squid with chili powder, salt, pepper, water and turmeric, stir, cover and cook on High for 15 minutes.
In your food processor, mix ginger with garlic, ginger and cumin and pulse really well.

Heat up a pan with the oil over medium high heat, add mustard seeds, toast them for 2 minutes and take off heat.

Release pressure from the pot, transfer squid and its liquid to the pan with the mustard seeds.

Add coconut paste as well, stir well, cook for a couple more minutes, divide on plates and serve.

Enjoy!

Simple Italian Braised Squid

It's a stylish Italian dish you will love for sure! Once you try it, this dish will become one of your favorite ones! We guarantee you that!

Preparation time: 6 minutes
Cooking time: 20 minutes
Servings: 4

Ingredients:

1 pound peas
1 pound squid, cut in medium pieces
1 yellow onion, chopped
½ pound tomatoes, crushed
1 tablespoon white wine
1 tablespoon olive oil
A pinch of sea salt
Black pepper to the taste

Directions:

Add the oil to your instant pot, set it on Sauté mode and heat it up.
Add onion, stir and cook for 3 minutes.
Add squid, stir and cook for 3 minutes more.
Add tomatoes, peas, wine, salt and pepper, stir, cover and cook on High for 15 minutes.
Release pressure, divide this on plates and serve.
Enjoy!

Magical Squid Dish

Can you believe you can make such a dish in your instant pot? This is really tasty and great!

Preparation time: 10 minutes
Cooking time: 25 minutes
Servings: 4

Ingredients:

1 small ginger piece, grated
10 garlic cloves, minced
1 pound squid, cut in medium pieces
2 yellow onions, chopped
2 green chilies, chopped
1 curry leaf
1 tablespoon coriander, ground
¼ cup coconut, shredded
½ tablespoon lemon juice
¾ tablespoon chili powder
A pinch of turmeric powder
A pinch of sea salt
Black pepper to the taste
1 teaspoon garam masala
1 teaspoon mustard seeds
3 tablespoons vegetable oil
¾ cup water

Directions:

Put the oil in your instant pot, set it on Sauté mode and heat it up.

Add mustard seeds, stir and toast them for 1 minute.Add coconut, stir and toast for 2 minutes more.

Add chilies, ginger, onions and garlic, stir and cook for 1 minute.

Add curry leaf, salt, pepper, lemon juice, coriander, chili powder, turmeric, garam masala, water and squid, stir, cover and cook on Low for 25 minutes.

Release pressure, divide into bowls and serve.

Enjoy!

Delicious Seafood Chowder

It's a great combination between a delicious gumbo and a tasty soup! This can't get any better! Try this amazing dish today!

Preparation time: 10 minutes
Cooking time: 15 minutes
Servings: 4

Ingredients:

1 cup yellow onion, chopped
1 pound shrimp
2 cups corn kernels
3 garlic cloves, minced
4 tablespoons butter
2 cups string beans, halved
2 cups carrots, chopped
8 ounces mushrooms, chopped
1 pound gold potatoes, cubed
Juice from 1 lemon
32 ounces chicken stock
¼ cup sherry
½ cup whipping cream
2 and ½ teaspoons celery seed
2 teaspoons parsley flakes
¼ teaspoon allspice
2 and ½ teaspoons mustard seeds, ground
1/8 teaspoon cardamom powder
1 teaspoon paprika

A pinch of cinnamon, ground

A pinch of ginger powder

A pinch of black pepper

A pinch of white pepper

A pinch of sea salt

A pinch of red pepper flakes

2 bay leaves

Directions:

Add butter to your instant pot, set it on Sauté mode, heat it up, add garlic and onions, stir and brown them for 2 minutes.

Add stock, corn, carrots, mushrooms, beans, potatoes, sherry and lemon juice and stir.

Also add celery seed, mustard seed, allspice, parsley flakes, cardamom, cinnamon, paprika, ginger, black pepper, white pepper, salt, pepper flakes and bay leaves and stir again.

Cover your instant pot and cook everything for 7 minutes.

Release pressure fast, add shrimp, stir, set the pot on Simmer mode and cook for a few more minutes.Add whipping cream, stir, divide into bowls and serve.

Enjoy!

Tasty Fish Soup

Find the right ingredients and get to work! You only need a few minutes to make this delicious soup that everyone will adore!

Preparation time: 5 minutes
Cooking time: 10 minutes
Servings: 4

Ingredients:

1 yellow onion, chopped
¾ cup bacon, chopped
2 celery ribs, chopped
2 garlic cloves, minced
1 carrot, minced
3 cups potatoes, cubed
2 tablespoons ghee
4 cups chicken stock
1 pound haddock fillets, chopped
White pepper to the taste
1 cup corn
2 cups heavy cream
1 tablespoon potato starch

Directions:

Set your instant pot on Sauté mode, add ghee and heat it up.
Add bacon, stir and cook until it's crispy.
Add celery, onion and garlic, stir and cook for 3 minutes.Add

white pepper, stock, corn, fish, potatoes, stir, cover and cook on High for 5 minutes.

Release pressure, add potato starch and cream, stir, set your pot to Simmer mode and cook for 3 minutes.

Divide into bowls and serve.

Enjoy!

Delicious Cod Soup

You must really try this great soup! This incredible recipe will take your breath away! Trust us!

Preparation time: 10 minutes
Cooking time: 25 minutes
Servings: 6

Ingredients:

4 cups red potatoes, cubed
½ cup mushrooms, chopped
2 tablespoons butter
1 cup onion, chopped
4 cups chicken stock
2 pound cod
1 teaspoon old bay seasoning
1 cup clam juice
1 cup water
½ cup flour
1 cup half and half
A pinch of sea salt

Directions:

Put the water in your instant pot, add the steamer basket inside, place the fish in the basket, cover and cook on high for 9 minutes.

Release pressure, transfer fish to a plate, chop and leave aside.

Clean your instant pot, add butter, set the pot on Sauté mode and melt it.

Add onion and mushrooms, stir and cook for 2 minutes.

Add stock, old bay seasoning, a pinch of salt and potatoes, stir, cover and cook on High for 8 minutes more.

Release pressure again, add fish, clam juice mixed with flour and half and half, stir well, divide into bowls and serve.

Enjoy!

Delicious Beans And Clams

This is very simple to make. It's a very flavored lunch or dinner idea! The seasoning is perfect and the combination of ingredients is amazing!

Preparation time: 10 minutes
Cooking time: 10 minutes
Servings: 6

Ingredients:

1 bay leaf
10 ounces canned white beans, drained
2 garlic cloves, minced
1 tablespoon olive oil
A pinch of salt
14 ounces clams
4 ounces white wine

Directions:

Put beans in your instant pot, add water to cover, a pinch of salt and bay leaf, stir, cover and cook on High for 10 minutes.
Release pressure, drain beans and clean your pot.
Add the oil to the pot, set it on Sauté mode and heat it up.
Add garlic, stir and cook for 2 minutes.
Add wine, beans and clams, stir, cover and cook on High for 6 minutes.
Release pressure, divide clams and beans in bowls and serve.
Enjoy!

Pasta With And Capers

You can never know to many tuna recipes! This is one very delicious one that can help you impress!

Preparation time: 10 minutes
Cooking time: 8 minutes
Servings: 4

Ingredients:

2 tablespoons capers
Water
11 ounces canned tuna in oil
Salt to the taste
16 ounces fussili pasta
2 cups tomato puree
1 garlic clove, minced
1 tablespoon olive oil
3 anchovies

Directions:

Put the oil in your instant pot, set it on Sauté mode and heat it up.
Add garlic and anchovies, stir and sauté them for 2 minutes.
Add salt, tomato puree, pasta and tuna and stir.
Add water to cover and cook on Low for 3 minutes.
Release pressure, divide tuna and pasta on plates and serve with capers on top.
Enjoy!

Special Tuna Casserole

You are going to love this incredible dish! It's so tasty and amazing and it will really surprise you!

Preparation time: 10 minutes
Cooking time: 4 minutes
Servings: 4

Ingredients:

2 and ½ cups macaroni pasta
10 ounces cream of mushrooms soup
3 cups water
14 ounces canned tuna, drained
A pinch of salt and black pepper
1 cup cheddar, cheese, shredded
1 cup peas

Directions:

In your instant pot, mix water with cream, tuna, macaroni, peas, salt and pepper, stir, cover and cook on High for 4 minutes.

Release pressure fast, add cheese, cover your pot and leave it aside for 5 minutes.

Divide tuna casserole on plates and serve.

Enjoy!

Simple Tuna Steaks

You can make this tonight for dinner if you are in the mood for something easy to make and super tasty!

Preparation time: 10 minutes
Cooking time: 5 minutes
Servings: 4

Ingredients:

4 medium tuna steaks
3 tablespoons lemon juice
2 tablespoons soy sauce
1/3 cup white wine
1 bunch fresh oregano
A pinch of salt and black pepper
Some lettuce and tomatoes salad for serving

Directions:

Put your tuna steaks in your instant pot, add soy sauce, lemon juice, wine, salt and pepper, add the steamer basket to the pot as well and put fresh oregano inside, cover pot and cook on High for 5 minutes.

Release pressure, uncover pot, divide tuna steaks and juices from the pot to plates and serve with lettuce and tomatoes salad on the side.

Enjoy!

Salmon Fillets And Delicious Sauce

These salmon fillets are going to help you make the best dinner for your loved ones and the sauce is a great addition!

Preparation time: 10 minutes
Cooking time: 6 minutes
Servings: 4

Ingredients:

4 salmon fillets
1 cup water
1 tablespoon lemon juice
3 tablespoons mayonnaise
1 teaspoon soy sauce
1 tablespoon dill, chopped
1 tablespoon brown sugar
2 tablespoons butter

Directions:

Put the water in your instant pot, place the steamer basket inside and add the fish to the basket.

Cover and cook on High for 5 minutes.

Meanwhile, put lemon juice, mayo, soy sauce, dill, sugar and butter in a pot, stir well and heat up over medium heat.

Release pressure from the pot, divide fish on plates and drizzle the sauce on top.

Enjoy!

Simple And Tasty Salmon

You only need 6 ingredients and 5 minutes to make a delicious salmon dish! The flavors will gain your heart and the whole dish will definitely amaze you!

Preparation time: 5 minutes
Cooking time: 5 minutes
Servings: 2

Ingredients:

2 salmon fillets
1 cup fish stock
1 tablespoons thyme, chopped
2 tablespoons mustard
1 bay leaf
Pink salt and black pepper to the taste

Directions:

In a bowl, mix mustard with thyme, salt and pepper and stir.
Rub salmon fillets with this mix.
Put the stock and the bay leaf in your instant pot, place the steamer basket inside and arrange salmon in the basket.
Cover and cook on High for 5 minutes.
Release pressure, divide salmon on plates and serve.
Enjoy!

Alex Baker

Simple Salmon And Onion Delight

It's a really simple dish! You can make this with only few ingredients! combine some simple tastes and obtain a marvelous result!

Preparation time: 10 minutes
Cooking time: 6 minutes
Servings: 4

Ingredients:

½ cup white wine
4 salmon steaks
1 yellow onion, sliced
1 lemon, sliced
½ cup water
Salt and black pepper to the taste

Directions:

Put the water, wine, some salt and pepper into your instant pot, stir and place the steamer basket inside.
Put salmon steaks in the basket, season with salt and pepper and cover them with onion and lemon slices.
Cook on High for 6 minutes, release pressure, divide fish, onion and lemon slices on top and serve right away.
Enjoy!

Teriyaki Salmon

This is a very special salmon delight you must enjoy with your loved ones as soon as possible!

Preparation time: 30 minutes
Cooking time: 10 minutes
Servings: 2

Ingredients:

¼ cup water
¼ cup mirin
2 salmon fillets
½ cup soy sauce
1 garlic clove, minced
1 tablespoon sesame oil
2 teaspoons sesame seeds
1 tablespoon ginger, grated
2 tablespoons brown sugar
1 cup water
3 green onions, chopped
1 tablespoons cornstarch mixed with 1 tablespoon water

Directions:

In a bowl, mix soy sauce with mirin, water, sesame oil, sesame seeds, ginger, garlic, green onions and brown sugar and stir well.
Add salmon, toss to coat, cover and keep in the fridge for 30 minutes.

Put 1 cup water to your instant pot and place the steamer basket inside.

Add a pan in the basket, put the salmon in the pan and reserve the marinade.

Cover your instant pot, cook on High for 8 minutes.

Meanwhile, put the marinade in a pot and heat it up over medium heat.

Add cornstarch mix, stir again well and cook until it thickens.

Release pressure from the pot, divide salmon on plates and drizzle the sauce on top.

Enjoy!

Delicious Sardines

Sardines are very easy to use and you can combine them in so many ways. Choose 10 sardines and make the most amazing dish with them.

Preparation time: 10 minutes
Cooking time: 12 minutes
Servings: 4

Ingredients:

10 ginger slices
2 tablespoons black vinegar
1 tablespoon soy sauce
1 umeboshi
3 ounces water
2 tablespoons sake
8 sardines

Directions:

In your instant pot, mix water with soy sauce, vinegar, ginger, umeboshi and sake and stir.
Add sardines on top, cover pot and cook on Low for 12 minutes.
Release pressure fast, divide sardines on plates, drizzle some of the sauce from the pot and serve.
Enjoy!

Amazing And Delicious Sardines

Sardines are easy to cook and they can be used in many dishes! This time, we recommend you a special combination of many tasty ingredients:

Preparation time: 15 minutes
Cooking time: 20 minutes
Servings: 5

Ingredients:

6 cloves
2 cups water
2 cups olive oil
Salt to the taste
2 pounds sardines
2 peppercorns
2 cups tomato sauce
1 carrot, chopped
2 bay leaves
1 pickle, sliced
1 red chili pepper, chopped
1 tablespoon sugar
1 tablespoon smoked paprika
10 garlic cloves

Directions:

Put sardines in a bowl, add the water over them and salt to the taste, leave them aside for 15 minutes, drain and put them in your instant pot.

Add oil, cloves, peppercorns, tomato sauce, carrot, bay leaves, chili pepper, pickle, sugar, paprika and garlic, stir gently, cover and cook on Low for 20 minutes.

Release pressure fast, divide everything on plates and serve.

Enjoy!

Mouthwatering Sardines

This incredible dish will make you so happy! It's light, delicious and easy to prepare at home if you have an instant pot!

Preparation time: 10 minutes
Cooking time: 15 minutes
Servings: 4

Ingredients:

1 pound sardines
2 yellow onions, cut in halves and then thinly sliced
8 garlic cloves, minced
1 inch ginger pieces, grated
1 green chili pepper, chopped
4 curry leaves
1 and ½ tablespoons chili powder
A pinch of sea salt
Black pepper to the taste
1 big tomato, chopped
½ teaspoon turmeric
3 tablespoons coconut oil
2 tablespoons white vinegar

Directions:

Put the oil in your instant pot, set it on Sauté mode and heat it up.
Add onion, ginger, garlic, chili and curry leaves, stir and cook

for 2 minutes.

Add chili powder, salt, pepper, tomato, turmeric and vinegar, stir well and cook for 3 minutes more.

Add sardines, cover your instant pot and cook on High for 10 minutes.

Release pressure, divide on plates and serve.

Enjoy!

Simple Lobster

Lobster tails are so delicious! We could eat as much as we can and never get sick of them! Did you know you could cook them in a very simple way in your instant pot?

Preparation time: 2 minutes
Cooking time: 3 minutes
Servings: 3

Ingredients:

2 pounds lobster tails
½ cup ghee, melted
1 cup water
A pinch of sea salt
Some black pepper

Directions:

Put the water in the pot,
Put lobster tails in the steamer basket and place this in the pot.
Cover and cook on High for 3 minutes.
Release pressure fast, transfer lobster tails to a bowl, drizzle melted ghee and sprinkle some salt and pepper.
Serve right away.
Enjoy!

Steamed Lobster

just steam a whole lobster in your instant pot and then make sure you enjoy it! It's so incredibly delicious!

Preparation time: 2 minutes
Cooking time: 3 minutes
Servings: 1

Ingredients:

1 cup beer
3 cups water
1 lobster
A pinch of sea salt
White pepper to the taste

Directions:

Put the water and the beer in your instant pot and place the steamer basket inside as well.
Put the lobster in the basket, cover and cook on High for 3 minutes.
Release pressure fast, transfer lobster to a platter and serve it with some salt and pepper on top.
Enjoy!

Great Lobster Bisque

You can serve this on a Sunday! This is just perfect: it's full of amazing and delicious ingredients that everyone will love!

Preparation time: 10 minutes
Cooking time: 7 minutes
Servings: 6

Ingredients:

30 ounces canned tomatoes, chopped
1 cup carrots, chopped
1 cup celery, chopped
1 tablespoon butter
2 shallots, chopped
1 garlic clove, crushed
32 ounces chicken stock
1 teaspoon dill, dried
1 tablespoon Italian seasoning
Black pepper to the taste
24 ounces lobster meat
5 teaspoons sweet paprika
1 pint heavy cream

Directions:

In a bowl, mix shallots with garlic and butter, stir and heat up in your microwave for 3 minutes.
Stir again and pour this into your instant pot.
Also add celery, tomatoes and carrots to the pot.

Add stock, paprika, black pepper and the lobster meat. Stir everything, cover and cook on High for 4 minutes.

Release pressure, blend your soup using an immersion blender, add cream, stir well, ladle into soup bowls and serve.

Enjoy!

Lobster And Potatoes

It's a really good dish made of ingredients you can easily find anywhere! Just make it tonight and see how tasty and flavored it is!

Preparation time: 10 minutes
Cooking time: 16 minutes
Servings: 4

Ingredients:

4 lobsters
2 garlic heads, not peeled
1 onion, cut in wedges
Water
Salt to the taste
1 and ½ pounds gold potatoes, peeled and halved
4 ears of corn, shucked and halved
4 tablespoons butter, melted

Directions:

Put potatoes in your instant pot.
Add garlic, onion, some salt and water to cover.
Cover your pot and cook on High for 12 minutes.
Release pressure, uncover, add lobsters and corn, cover again and cook on High for 5 minutes more.
Release pressure again, divide potatoes and corn on plates, season them with salt and drizzle some of the butter over them.

Discard onion and garlic, transfer lobsters to a cutting board and take meat out.

Divide it on plates next to potatoes and corn, drizzle the rest of the butter over them, sprinkle some salt and serve.

Enjoy!

Thai Red Snapper

This is an exotic dish that requires your full attention! You need a lot of ingredients and you need to combine them perfectly! You will obtain a rich dish everyone will adore!

Preparation time: 30 minutes
Cooking time: 20 minutes
Servings: 2

Ingredients:

For the marinade:
1 tablespoon fish sauce
1 cup coconut milk
1 tablespoon Thai curry paste
Zest from 1 lime
Juice from ½ lime
2 teaspoons brown sugar
1 tablespoon ginger, grated
1 teaspoon garlic, minced
2 red snapper fillets
1 lime, sliced
2 cups water
1 tablespoon cilantro, chopped
For the salsa:
2 mangoes, peeled and chopped
2 jalapenos, chopped
1 scallions, chopped
A handful cilantro, chopped

Juice from 1 lime

Directions:

In a bowl, mix fish sauce with coconut milk, curry paste, zest from 1 lime, juice from ½ lime, brown sugar, ginger and garlic and whisk well.

Add fish fillets, toss to coat and leave aside for 30 minutes.

Meanwhile, in another bowl, mix mangos with jalapenos, scallion, a handful cilantro and juice from 1 lime, stir well and leave aside.

Put the water in your instant pot and place the steamer basket inside.

Put fish fillets in 2 parchment paper pieces, cover them with lime slices and wrap them.

Place them in the steamer basket, cover the pot and cook on High for 10 minutes.

Release pressure, divide fish on plates and leave aside for now.

Put the marinade from the fish into a pan and heat it up over medium high heat.

Boil from a couple of minutes and take off heat.

Drizzle some of the sauce over dish, top with the mango salsa and sprinkle cilantro on top.

Enjoy!

Delicious Red Snapper And Tomato Sauce

If you are looking for an easy fish recipe you can cook tonight in your instant pot, then this is the best one! It's going to be ready in a few minutes and it will taste wonderful!

Preparation time: 10 minutes
Cooking time: 7 minutes
Servings: 4

Ingredients:

4 medium red snapper fillets
A pinch of saffron threads
3 tablespoons hot water
1 yellow onion, chopped
¼ cup olive oil
A pinch of sea salt
Black pepper to the taste
16 ounces canned tomatoes, crushed
2 tablespoons parsley
4 ciabatta rolls, cut in halves and toasted

Directions:

In a bowl, mix saffron with hot water and leave aside for now.
Set your instant pot on Sauté mode, add the oil and heat it up.
Add onion, stir and cook for 2 minutes.Add fish, cook for 2

minutes and flip on the other side.

Add tomatoes, drained saffron, some salt and pepper, cover the pot and cook on Low for 5 minutes.

Release pressure, divide fish and sauce on plates, sprinkle parsley and serve with ciabatta rolls on the side.

Enjoy!

Baked Red Snapper

We know this might sound strange but trust us: you can bake some red snapper in your instant pot! Pay attention and learn how to do so!

Preparation time: 30 minutes
Cooking time: 12 minutes
Servings: 4

Ingredients:

4 red snappers, cleaned
½ cup olive oil
½ cup parsley, chopped
5 garlic cloves, minced
A pinch of sea salt
Black pepper to the taste
4 tablespoons lemon juice
5 ounces grape leaves, blanched
1 lemon, sliced
2 cups water

Directions:

Pat dry fish and put it in a bowl.
Season with salt, pepper and brush with half the oil, rub well and keep in the fridge for 30 minutes.
In a bowl mix garlic with salt, pepper and parsley and stir.
Divide this into fish cavities, wrap each in grape leaves, drizzle the lemon juice over them and place in a heat proof

dish that fits your steamer basket.

Drizzle the rest of the oil over fish, cover dish with some tin foil, place the basket inside the pot and arrange the dish in the basket.

Add 2 cups water to your instant pot, cover and cook on High for 12 minutes.

Release pressure, divide wrapped fish on plates and top with lemon slices.

Enjoy!

Red Snapper And Chili Sauce

This is a Korean style recipe you can easily make at home! So, don't wait too long and bring Korean tastes into your kitchen!

Preparation time: 30 minutes
Cooking time: 12 minutes
Servings: 2

Ingredients:

1 red snapper, cleaned
3 tablespoons Korean chili paste
A pinch of sea salt
2 teaspoons sugar
1 tablespoon soy sauce
1 garlic clove, minced
½ teaspoon ginger, grated
2 teaspoons Korean plum extract
2 teaspoons sesame seeds, toasted
1 teaspoon sesame oil
1 green onion, chopped
2 cups water

Directions:

Make some slits into your fish, season with some salt and leave aside for 30 minutes.

Put the water in your instant pot, add the steamer basket inside and place the fish in it.

Rub fish with the chili paste, cover your instant pot and cook on Low for 12 minutes.

Meanwhile, in a bowl, mix sugar with soy sauce, garlic, ginger, plum extract, sesame seeds, sesame oil and green onion and stir very well.

Release pressure from the pot, divide fish on plates and serve with the sauce you've made on top.

Enjoy!

Spicy Anchovies

This spicy and delicious dish is both exotic and original! You will discover some interesting ingredients in this dish! So, go get your ingredients and get to work!

Preparation time: 10 minutes
Cooking time: 4 minutes
Servings: 2

Ingredients:

2 garlic cloves, minced
1 tablespoon gochujang
1 tablespoon water
1 tablespoon sugar
1 cup anchovies, dried
1 tablespoon sesame seed oil
½ tablespoon vegetable oil
Black sesame seeds for serving
Roasted sesame seeds for serving

Directions:

In a bowl, mix gochujang with water, garlic and sugar, stir and leave aside for a couple of minutes.

Set your instant pot on Sauté mode, add anchovies, stir, cook them for 1 minute and transfer to a bowl

Add vegetable oil, stir and heat up for 1 minute more.

Add gochujang mix, stir, cover and cook on High for 2 minutes.

Release pressure, add anchovies to the pot, sesame oil, black sesame seeds and roasted ones, stir well, transfer to 2 serving bowl and serve.

Enjoy!

Alex Baker

Calamari And Tomatoes

You can serve this as a main course or as a side dish! It's a very versatile dish! You'll see!

Preparation time: 5 minutes
Cooking time: 30 minutes
Servings: 4

Ingredients:

15 ounces canned tomatoes, chopped
1 and ½ pounds calamari, cleaned, heads detached, tentacles separated and cut in thin strips
1 garlic clove, minced
½ cup white wine
1 bunch parsley, chopped
A pinch red pepper flakes
2 anchovies, chopped
Juice from 1 lemon
A drizzle of olive oil
A pinch of sea salt
Black pepper to the taste

Directions:

Set the instant pot on Sauté mode, add the oil and heat it up.
Add garlic, anchovies and pepper flakes, stir and cook for 3 minutes.
Add calamari, stir and sauté them for 5 minutes more.Add wine, stir and cook for 3 minutes more.

Add tomatoes, half of the parsley, some salt and pepper, stir, cover and cook on High for 20 minutes.

Release the pressure, add lemon juice and the rest of the parsley, stir, divide on plates and serve.

Enjoy!

Salmon Cheesecake

This is perfect for a party! It's such an interesting and unique dish that everyone will love for sure!

Preparation time: 10 minutes
Cooking time: 25 minutes
Servings: 4

Ingredients:

For the base:
6 ounces oatcakes, crushed
2 ounces butter, melted
For the cheesecake:
8 ounces smoked salmon, flaked
1 tablespoon parsley, chopped
1 tablespoon dill, chopped
16 ounces cream cheese
½ tablespoon chives, chopped
2 cups water
Some grated cheddar cheese
4 eggs
1 tablespoon sour cream
3 tablespoons parmesan cheese, grated
Juice from 1 lemon

Directions:

In a bowl mix oatcakes with melted butter and stir well.Press this into a lined cake pan that fits your instant pot.

In a blender, mix cream cheese with cheddar, sour cream, eggs, parsley, dill, salmon, chives, lemon juice and parm and pulse really well.

Spread this over the base, cover with tin foil, place in the steamer basket of your pot.

Add 2 cups water to the pot, cover and cook on Manual for 20 minutes.

Release pressure, leave cheesecake to cool down, slice and serve it.

Enjoy!

Shrimp Dumplings

These are so flavored, crunchy and delicious! It's a satisfying meal that everyone will love!

Preparation time: 10 minutes
Cooking time: 10 minutes
Servings: 24

Ingredients:

½ pound tiger shrimp, peeled, deveined and chopped
1 tablespoon cornstarch+ 1 teaspoon cornstarch
A pinch of sea salt
Black pepper to the taste
½ teaspoon olive oil
½ pound pork, ground
2 tablespoons chicken stock
1 tablespoon shaoxing wine
1 teaspoon soy sauce
1 teaspoon fish sauce
1 teaspoon sesame oil
½ teaspoon sugar
1 green onion stack, chopped
2 shiitake mushrooms, chopped
2 ginger slices, chopped
24 wonton wrappers
2 cups water

Directions:

In a bowl, mix shrimp with 1 teaspoon cornstarch, salt and pepper, stir well and leave aside for now.

In another bowl, mix pork with 1 tablespoon cornstarch, salt, pepper, sugar, wine, soy sauce, chicken stock, fish sauce and sesame oil and stir well.

Combine the 2 mixtures and stir very well.

Add green onions, ginger and mushrooms and stir well again.

Shape 24 balls out of this mix and wrap each in a wonton wrapper.

Place balls in the steamer basket, add 2 cups water to your instant pot and place the basket inside.

Cover and cook on High for 10 minutes.

Release pressure fast, transfer shrimp dumplings on plates and serve.

Enjoy!

Delicious Conch Soup

It's going to be a big surprise for everyone when you serve them this seafood dish! Everyone will want to know the secret of your successful dish!

Preparation time: 5 minutes
Cooking time: 20 minutes
Servings: 4

Ingredients:

1 red sweet bell pepper, chopped
2 green bell peppers, chopped
3 cups water
4 celery stick, chopped
1 brown onion, chopped
4 conchs
A pinch of sea salt
Black pepper to the taste

Directions:

Put conch on a working surface, pound with a meat pounder and chop.

Put conch pieces in your instant pot, add water to cover and cook on High for 10 minutes.

Release pressure, discard water and add the 2 cups of clean water.

Also add salt, pepper, celery, red and green bell peppers and onion.

Stir, cover and cook on High for 10 minutes.

Release pressure, ladle soup into bowls and serve.
Enjoy!

Conclusion

This amazing recipes collection is the best you'll ever have! Itdoesn't get any better, even if you search all over, you cannot get acookbook better than this.

You now have the opportunity to cook some of the best and mostdelicious instant pot seafood and fish recipes ever! Sincerely, youwill impress your family, friends and guests with your cookingskills.

"Instant Pot Fish & Seafood Cookbook: 77 Healthy& DeliciousInstant Pot Recipes for Your Family" is the ultimate instant potfish and seafood cooking guide!So, get your hands on a copy and start cooking your irresistiblefish and seafood!Truly, you will have so much fun in the kitchen from now on!

Made in the USA
San Bernardino, CA
27 December 2018